# Open House Hacks:

# Pro Tips, Ideas, & Tricks to Help You Plan It Like a **Rock Star**!

By Pam Zentner

© 2016   Pam Zentner

All rights reserved. No part of this publication may be reproduced, distributed, or transmitted in any form or by any means, including photocopying, recording, or other electronic or mechanical methods, without the prior written permission of the publisher, except in the case of brief quotations embodied in critical reviews and certain other noncommercial uses permitted by copyright law. For permission requests, write to the publisher, addressed "Attention: Permissions Coordinator," at the address below.

Pam Zentner
Zentner & Company
PO Box 950141
Atlanta, Georgia 30377

# Table of Contents

Dedication .................................................................................. iv
Preface ....................................................................................... v
Before Your Open House ........................................................ 1
    Selecting the Perfect Property ........................................... 2
    Contacting the Listing Agent .............................................. 3
    Activate Your Marketing Campaign ................................. 6
During Your Open House ...................................................... 10
    What to Bring ....................................................................... 11
    What to Do With Your Hands ............................................ 13
After Your Open House ......................................................... 15
    Remember Your Manners .................................................. 16
    Guest Care ............................................................................. 17
Resources ................................................................................. 18
    The Checklist to Make Life Easier ..................................... 19
    OH Emergency Supplies Box ............................................. 21
Notes ......................................................................................... 22

## Dedication

He sits at countless open houses protecting me from the potential perils of the outside world.

He drags heavy boxes full of "important stuff I can't live without" to and from my car every weekend.

He supports every decision I make, even after thoroughly investigating all options and running multiple ROI calculations himself.

He rescues me when I lock myself IN a house and can't get out OR when my car breaks down on the other side of town OR when I get lost in the big city and can't find my way home OR when I'm one phone call away from running away screaming up the street! He's my calm.

He wrestles with countless signs, flags, and wayward household appliances without even a second thought. He even drives around town collecting those signs at the end of my open houses so I can get home faster.

He happily and eagerly accepts texts throughout his work day simply bearing an address and the contact information of strangers…and he's ready to act upon that if needed.

Without the unyielding support of my husband, Jack, the adventures of this fun, exciting career would be impossible for me to tackle…and much less fun!

# Preface

I have no intentions of arguing for or against the value of hosting open houses. Agents have their own experiences and ideas about this business-building strategy, so if you've decided to host, this book is for you! It's my assumption going in that you want to plan a successful open house, and through this short book I'll help you realize that goal.

I've written this book as an informational guide for new and seasoned agents alike. This book is not intended to be Open House training but instead a continuation of the training you've received from your broker thus far.

I've compiled the best tips, ideas, and tricks I use regularly when planning open houses. Several of these ideas are often overlooked. I receive accolades from other agents who visit my open houses when they look at the materials I've prepared.

It's my hope that you'll read through this book and have at least one "ah ha" moment! Read it, and read it again. Use it as a checklist when you begin planning your next OH.

New agents, here's the magic that will set you apart as a true professional.

Seasoned agents, it's my hope you'll get several new ideas to add to your Open House Toolbox.

It's not my intent for you to do EVERY thing in here; start with something new and build upon it. Take the ideas and customize them to your own business. Share the ideas with a colleague.

When you're finished, please contact me to tell me how you enjoyed it. I'd love to hear your favorite OH tricks too!
Pam@ZentnerAndCompany.com

# Before Your Open House

> "Plans are nothing.
> Planning is everything."
>
> ~ Dwight D. Eisenhower

Preparing for the open house will take a considerable amount of effort the first go-around or two. But it becomes much easier once you become accustomed to the routine. I really enjoy the planning phase of my open houses; it allows me to be creative but also to track a variety of strategies and techniques.

To make things easier, I've created for myself a checklist that I use as soon as I find a property I want to host. I don't do every item on the list, but it has become my essential guide during my planning stage. If you write down everything you do with every open house, you'll begin to see a pattern and will create your own checklist. Doing this allows you to stay on track more easily while also allowing more time for new ideas. I highly recommend some type of organized planning routine with every OH. To get you started, I've included in the RESOURCES section a checklist of the material covered in this book.

## Selecting the Perfect Property

This sounds simple enough, right? Well, it's not! When selecting your host property, you'll need to keep several things in mind: your target location; the parking situation; price point; the sell-ability of the property; ease of access.

You certainly want to pick a property that fits your standards. So if your target is a specific area, go there. If your target is single family detached homes, don't look for a condo. Stick to the price point that your preferred client falls into.

You also want to pay attention to the parking situation for an open house. Living in a large metropolitan area has its limitations on open house day. The streets here can be very crowded with pedestrians, so choosing a location where visitors have to struggle with parking can limit visitor numbers. Take your area's unique features into consideration when choosing a house to host.

My best advice here is to visit your prospective property before choosing it! I search for a handful of potentials on my company's site. After finding a few possibilities, I go look at them. There's nothing worse than showing up for your open house only to discover that dreaded "cat smell!" Many times, properties will eliminate themselves with a quick visit; don't skip this part!

## Contacting the Listing Agent

My broker has an amazing way of allowing agents to share listings. New agents can benefit from the company's listings by simply hosting for another agent. If you're not sure if you have access to this type of arrangement, just ask your broker.

Nonetheless, if you don't have a listing of your own yet, you'll need to "borrow" one from someone. So prepare your begging speech and pick up the phone!

When you get the listing agent, you'll need to discuss a few things: getting permission to host their listing; explaining your marketing strategy; finding out about HOA and/or owner restrictions; asking the listing agent to update the listing online.

**Call the listing agent and ask for permission to host the open house and give highlights about your marketing plans.**
Be prepared to offer up some of your marketing plans so they trust you know what you're doing! Reassuring the listing agent that you have a good knowledge base of what to do will go a long way. You don't have to go over everything, but give him a broad idea of your plans for the OH. Most agents are happy for extra help. Chances are, he'll need to clear it with his seller before committing to you at this stage, so allow for eventuality in your plans.

Don't get discouraged, though, if you're told no a few times. I've been told no more times than I've been told yes. Remember it's not you; it's not personal...perhaps the seller has limitations. Just remember to keep moving and keep asking.

**Speak to the listing agent about any restrictions associated with the property.**
Be sure to ask him about HOA restrictions, especially regarding signs and marketing materials. If you are allowed to put signs up only during the OH, do it as instructed. If you're not allowed signs at all, no signs should be placed. Sometimes I've hosted in communities that won't allow door knocking; I had to mail

invitations to the neighbors. Find out the restrictions and work around them.

If the property is in a gated community, ask about guest access during your OH. Some communities will allow the gate to open during your open house hours; some communities will allow a call be placed to you instead of the owner during that time period. You should know what's expected and follow through to make that happen BEFORE your OH. There's no worse stress than rolling in to you OH to realize at that point you didn't plan for this! Visiting the property beforehand will give you great information about how you should prepare for the day.

Asking about seller preferences is also a great idea. Find out if the seller has any concerns about an open house and be sure to do what you can to put him at ease about this.

**Ask the listing agent to add your OH your local MLS.**
The agents in my office are members of two different local multiple listing services. Each service allows us to update listing information to indicate an upcoming open house. When I ask, I also include any secondary consumer sites I use myself, such as Zillow, Trulia, Realtor.com in the request. Often, the listing agent is taking notes, so I try to be organized with my conversation to help them out in the process.

I ask the listing agent to do this for me; otherwise, for a multitude of business reasons, they may not think about doing it. I consider this my responsibility as the host, not theirs. Of course, I don't have access to the listing of another agent, so I can't add it myself, but I do ask and if it's not done, I send a nice reminder a few days before the open house. There are typically several communications between the hosting and listing agents before an open house, and this is just one (if needed).

**Once you've gotten permission to host**, be prepared to follow the agent's instructions to the letter! If you're told no food is to be served at the open house, don't serve food at the open house! If you're told to turn off the lights, turn off the lights. Write down everything and remember to be a good steward of the trust instilled in you for the afternoon. Listing agents have to answer to their clients, so don't put them in the position of having to explain something out of their control.

You'll eventually earn street cred in your office and build trust with your fellow agents. Then, before you know it, you'll be the agent they call every time they get a new listing!

Turnabout is fair play! Don't forget to return the favor when you have listings. There will be some new go-getting agent in your office just dying to scrape up new clients; help 'em out! We're all in this together, and we all have the same goal of getting our clients to the closing table so they can start their new life in their beautiful new home. Helping each other is one of the best parts of this business!

## Activate Your Marketing Campaign

**Digital marketing** is how you'll find people online. As you already know, people spend way too much time online. Go there and get them to visit your open house!

This is where Zillow, Trulia, Realtor.com, and your local MLS listing information will help. Home buyers begin their search online, so doesn't it make sense to let them know there about your open house?

It's imperative to use all your social outlets to announce and send reminders about your open house. I start a couple weeks before with a little announcement. Then as time goes on, I release different details about the home I'm hosting. I always include the date/time of my OH and my contact information with the request to reach out to me for more information. I don't always include the price or the exact location, unless I'm targeting other agents (they need to know so they can plan client visits). But when I'm targeting the general public, I want them to contact me to get the deets...otherwise they know and don't need me. I want them to need me!

I plan and create Facebook ads that target a very specific audience based upon the location and price of the property, particularly household income that would allow a mortgage approval for the price point. This can be a very lengthy process so taking the time to learn about FB ads will benefit you here. If you don't care about FB ads, don't worry about learning it. Easy enough, right?

After I've created open house flyers, I convert them to JPGs and PDFs so I can share everywhere: Linkedin, Instagram, FB, Twitter, Google+, and my blog (PamZentner.wordpress.com).

Don't post JUST ONCE. Post several times throughout the course of your planning period. You might also consider creating an event on Facebook and "boosting" that to generate interest. Don't just regurgitate the same post again and again though; create new posts with different information and different photos each time if possible.

The key is persistence and creativity when posting online. Be catchy but not kitschy.

I believe **print marketing** is essential when marketing an open house, and I use a variety of avenues to do this.

You simply MUST begin with creating a fantastic property flyer. From here you'll have lots more choices. I use this property flyer in a million ways (not literally a million but quite a lot)!

Work with a lender who will create the financials for the property. My affiliated lender actually creates the flyer for me once I've shared the property listing information with them. They include all the financial particulars, which makes it easy for me to target potential buyers (including current homeowners and even potential first-time buyers) who will meet these criteria.

I don't waste the back of my property flyer. How many times have you gone to an open house, picked up the property information, left, and read over the materials later? Everyone does that; take advantage of this by creating a short, enticing "bio" on the back of the flyer. I include information about why a client should pick me over other agents and my contact information in SUPER LARGE print. Use your creativity here; you're selling yourself, so don't be shy. Do, however, keep it simple. You don't want to create a page full of small text. Create a flyer-type info sheet highlighting you as the best choice. And make your (high res) photo nice and large! You are your brand, so don't skimp here.

Once my flyer is as awesome as I need it to be, the magic begins.

I use my local MLS to locate local renters (hopefully they will become first-time home buyer clients) who would fit the mortgage requirements. I invite them to the OH using my fantastic property flyer. I do this by searching for rental properties with a lease set to expire within the next month or two. I mail them a copy of the flyer.

I use my local MLS to locate potential buyers who would fit the mortgage requirements (based on their current home value...think "move up" buyers). I invite them to the OH using my fantastic property flyer.

Canvass the neighborhood and invite the neighbors; they are usually a great source of information about who wants to move in. They have friends and family who want to move. Don't ignore them! You have a couple options here based upon your personal preference. You can knock on the doors, you can drop off, or you can mail to them. Be sure to check with the HOA to learn of any restrictions about this.

If you knock on the doors of the neighbors, be sure to have something to hand them (how about a fantastic property flyer?). Have a quick script prepared so you don't freeze up when the door is opened. Tell them about your open house and ask them if they know anyone who wants to move into the neighborhood. Keep the visit short and give them something valuable (offer them a free home value analysis?).

The same basic concept applies if you're dropping something off; you simply drop off something without knocking on the door. Door hangers are a perfect invitation in this case. Simply place the door hanger and leave. Another idea is to order door bags and put your flyer and a small trinket in there before hanging it on the door. In my bags I place the property flyer invitation and some company marketing materials. I've also ordered and used personalized candy boxes filled with hard candy...I don't personalize these with the OH information so it would be beneficial to attach the flyer to it. A note here: some door knobs don't allow a way of simply hanging a bag on it, so I carry a spool of ribbon and a pair of scissors in my bag when I'm hanging bags or treats on doors. Then I can tie the ribbon through the hole in the bag and around a part of the door knob. Experience is a brutal teacher.

Mailing the flyer to the neighbors is always an option too. When I choose this option, I choose to do it BIG by using the USPS's EDDM tool. If you don't know about this already, investigate it! It will change how you mail for your business! (I'm creating an informational book on this too. I've taught several small learning groups and all agents can certainly benefit.) Basically you can target a large mail route (200+ doors in some cases) for a fraction of the cost of a first-class stamp! Check on size requirements and allow yourself enough time for design...and be prepared to take your flyers, en masse, to the correct post office.

And of course, few days before your event, strategically place your OH signs. Know your city's sign ordinance. This is when you'll be glad you spoke to the listing agent about the HOA's sign restrictions because your signs will get picked up if you don't follow the rules. Many agents utilize balloons on their signs to draw attention; I don't. Go read about Helium! It's a limited, non-renewable resource. I choose to NOT squander it in such a way. <PREACH> I do use large flags branded with my broker's logo in the OH front yard. I know other agents who use pinwheels to draw attention to their signs. The important point here is to get your signs out so people driving by will know about your open house, too! You do it YOUR way.

## During Your Open House

"Thinking will not overcome fear but action will."

~ W. Clement Stone

What to do during an open house can be a little intimidating, but don't let that fear keep you from hosting! There are buyers out there, go get them!

## What to Bring

Some days when I show up to an open house, it looks like I'm moving in!

However, what I bring is basically very simple: my computer bag, purse, and OH Emergency Supply Kit.

My **computer bag** is stuffed with documents and marketing materials. I've discovered the importance of having lots of marketing materials about myself and my company...and I readily hand it out to everyone who walks through the door.

I bring contract documents partially completed. If someone wants to buy today; I'll be ready. Of course I have an online workspace I most certainly utilize but I plan for the possibility the technology may be on the fritz.

I never show up to an OH without Buyer Brokerage Agreements! I've seen some agents who have placed them on the counter with the marketing materials, but I keep them handy but out of sight. Personal preference. Have some with you.

I have lots of extra property flyers.

I bring extra copies of the Client Copy of the MLS printout for the property, just in case there aren't any at the home already.

I bring work I can do during periods of inactivity. I don't ask for the wi-fi password because I can use my phone as a hotspot. But if you foresee needing an internet connection, be sure to ask your listing agent beforehand so you'll be prepared when you arrive.

I create and bring a professional-looking binder with information relevant to your buyer guests. This binder has the property information for the current OH property and information about other comps in the neighborhood and surrounding area. In here, my guests will find zoned schools and other interesting nearby attractions. This binder is very organized and divided. I prop it up right in the middle of all the home information so the guests can see there's more to see! Nothing like a little danglin' carrot!

I bring current copies of relevant "Home" magazines.

I always have an easy method for registering every guest (Google forms, prize drawings, paper pad). Every guest who enters the home must sign in. I prefer Google forms for its ease, but you'll need to become very accustomed to it beforehand or risk seeming like a buffoon as you struggle with it in front of your guests! Otherwise have a registration pad and lots of pens.

I sometimes offer small giveaways (branded keychains, koozies, stress balls, etc). This is not necessary but can be appealing to guests and can encourage them to sign in.

My **Open House Emergency Supply Kit** is full of things I've discovered might be essential in a pinch. You can find my complete list in the RESOURCES section at the end of this book.

Many agents like to bake cookies or brownies or host wine & cheese galas! I don't do any of that! I'm a hot mess most days, so just getting here with the essentials is an accomplishment. My main reason for skipping this is *liability*: I don't want to explain the new stain on the carpet or why there's a cookie stuck to the duvet cover or why the pan is warped after I forget and let the cookies burn. It's too big a burden for me, and I recommend you skipping this too. At the very least, speak to your listing agent (or seller if you're the listing agent) and get permission. But remember no amount of permission can clear you if some poor child gets a sucker lodged in their throat! Food is dangerous; I don't do it. However, I have hosted a broker open with food and beverage; that's a different animal for a different day.

## What to Do With Your Hands

This is the scary part! ...not really but it can be frightening when people start arriving and you have no idea what's going on. Here are a couple ideas to ward off that stage fright.

Know what you're going to say and practice beforehand. If you **have a script**, use it. I keep mine very simple.

Be friendly! **Greet every guest** upon their entering the home **but don't hover** over them the whole time, unless that's be requested by the seller.

Allow the guest a few minutes to walk around then **go check on them** to answer questions and point out great features of the home. I say something like, "What do you think about these heart of pine floors?" Get them talking about themselves and what they're looking for without sounding like you're interrogating them. Be comfortable so they'll be comfortable.

I've been to many open houses and I can tell you this part, as logical as it seems, is most often skipped by the hosting agent: **ASK FOR THE SALE!** After all the guest is looking at homes for sale, so JUST MAYBE they might be willing to buy a house! Right?? Say something light and breezy like, "So what do you think? Is this your next home?" Even if it's not, I guarantee you'll get some important information from them about what they want; write it down!

Thank your guests for coming and promise to follow up with them. Then follow up with them! Sometimes the follow up is immediately. I've had guests schedule time with me immediately following my OH...meaning when they visited they liked homes in my Buyer Binder, so I called and made appointments for the time following my open house and I met them there when I closed up shop. Don't be afraid to ask! If you don't ask, the answer is no. If you do, it could be yes.

The important this to remember is be busy! Much of your time will be filled hosting but much of your time will be idle if you don't plan something into it. Over plan for this time and get work done, even if it's returning emails. If you sit still, you'll get nervous and second guess yourself.

# After Your Open House

"Action is the foundational key to all success."

~ Pablo Picasso

## Remember Your Manners

Don't just gather your stuff and go. Be responsible and clean up your mess. If you had lunch while hosting the open house, clean up the mess. Don't leave drink cans sitting around. If you used your listing agent's marketing material as a coaster, at least have the decency to throw it away instead of putting it back in her literature holder. Go through the house to make sure everything's locked up and back in place as well as you can.

And know that now's where the "real" work begins: fostering the relationships you began today!

Remember to remove all your signs and balloon debris if you used balloons. Leaving pieces of balloons and/or ribbon really ticks off the neighbors, so don't do it.

When you get back to the office, send a quick email to the listing agent informing her of your experience. Be sure to detail any difficulty or trouble that you experienced during the open house but be sure to focus on the positive experience you had due to her allowing you to host her listing. You're trying to build a positive business relationship, so be professional.

Also hand-write a "thank you" card to your donating agent. Be genuine when telling her how much you appreciate the trust she had in you and say something nice about your experience. Send it to her at her office.

## Guest Care

Following up with your guests is important. Add them all to your database. Follow up with each guest as soon as possible. I spend the morning after my open house creating digital thank you cards. I send one to everyone, inviting them to let me know how I can help.

If a particular guest seemed particularly ready to move forward, send them addition properties after running a search for them. Be sure to focus your energy on the people who you feel are ready to buy; you want to convert them as quickly as possible.

Within a few days of the OH, give each guest a call "check in." This is a great time to ask any questions you might have forgotten during the busy open house. Use this opportunity to sell yourself to them again…nothing too pressure-filled but certainly offer to help them and tell them why you think you're a great choice. Make an appointment as soon as possible! They're looking at houses, go show them houses. You can't sell homes if you're not showing them, so ask for the appointment.

Each guest should also be added to an appropriate drip campaign to ensure future communication.

# Resources

# The Checklist to Make Life Easier

## Before the Open House
- Select the property (location, ease of access, fits your preferred price range, sellable)
- If you're not the listing agent, contact for permission to host.
- Speak to the listing agent about your marketing plans and ask about any restrictions (HOA, owner's needs, etc)
- Ask the listing agent to add your OH to Zillow, Trulia, and other local OH sites, specifically your local MLS.
- Begin your marketing campaign (print and digital).
- Locate local renters who would fit the mortgage requirements and invite them to the OH.
- Locate local potential buyers and invite them to the OH.
- Canvass the neighborhood and invite the neighbors.
- A few days before, place your OH signs.

## During the Open House
- Bring an emergency kit of likely needed materials.
- Bring important marketing materials about yourself and your company.
- Bring a professional-looking binder with information relevant to your buyer guests.
- Bring work you can do during periods of inactivity.
- I never have food! I don't want to be held liable for stains or messes.
- I also never use balloons because helium is a limited, non-renewable resource.
- Have an easy method for registering every guest (Google forms, prize drawings, paper pad)
- I sometimes offer small giveaways (keychains, koozies, stress balls, etc). This is not necessary but can be appealing to guests.
- Know what you're going to say and practice beforehand.
- Greet every guest upon their entering the home but don't hover.

- Allow the guest a few minutes to walk around then go check on them to answer questions and point out great features.
- ASK FOR THE SALE!
- Thank your guests for coming and promise to follow up with them

**After the Open House**
- Remember to remove all your signs and balloon debris if you used balloons.
- Hand-write a "thank you" card to your donating agent.
- Add your guests to your database.
- Give each guest a call a couple days after the OH to "check in."
- Follow up with each guest (thank you note for attending OH, send new search results, updates on the OH property, etc)
- Add each guest to an appropriate drip campaign.

## OH Emergency Supplies Box

- Pair of scissors
- Spool of ribbon
- Roll of paper towels
- Toilet tissue
- All-purpose cleaner
- Rubber gloves
- Small hand broom and dustpan
- Roll of painter's tape
- Lint roller
- Air freshener
- Small travel sewing kit
- Hammer (don't ask) ☺  ...but for pounding in signs, of course

# Notes

Thank you so much for taking the time to read *Open House Hacks: Pro Tips, Ideas, & Tricks to Help You Plan It Like a Rock Star!*

If you enjoyed this book, please give it a great review! And encourage your friends to order it too.

Look for more titles coming soon from Pam Zentner, including:
- Using EDDM to Build Your Business
- Surviving My 1st Year in Real Estate Was NO Piece of Cake: One REALTOR'S Humorous Look Back

Pam encourages your ideas and comments. You can email her at Pam@ZentnerAndCompany.com.

Are you a SOCIAL BUTTERFLY too? Connect with Pam in as many ways as you'd like.
http://www.facebook.com/AtlantaITPDreamHomes

http://www.linkedin.com/in/atlantaitpdreamhomes

http://twitter.com/PamZentnerRE

http://www.instagram.com/realtorpamzentner

http://www.pamzentner.wordpress.com

www.ingramcontent.com/pod-product-compliance
Lightning Source LLC
Chambersburg PA
CBHW071835200526
45169CB00018B/1521